MY EMOTIONAL PLEAS......

is a personal catharsis

composite of poems......

....art

....music.

to enlighten . . .

to laugh . . . .

to cry . . .

TO EVOLVE.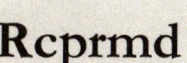

..   **Rcprmd**

MY EMOTIONAL PLEAS

When looking at you, what a doctor sees.

By Rapper MD.

Copyright © 2010 by RapperMD

All rights reserved. No part of this book may be used or reproduced in any manner whatsoever without the written permission except in the case of short excerpts or quotations cited appropriately. For additional information, contact Rapper Md @ mula@prodigy.net or the address below.

Nieferxis Creative Works
5116 Bissonnet St. #459
Bellaire Texas, 77401

Library of Congress Control Number: (2010---------------)
ISBN: 9780984424702

Printed in the United States of America.

First Edition, March 2010

The book may be bulk ordered at special rates.
Contact RapperMD @ mula@prodigy.net or write to Nieferxis Creative Works, 5116 Bissonnet St. #459. Bellaire Texas 77401.

MY

EMOTIONAL

PLEAS

When looking at you, what a doctor sees

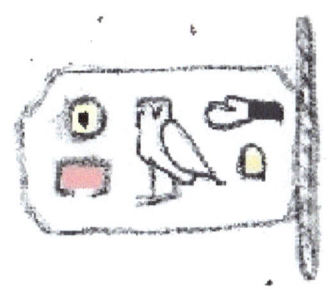

By RapperMD

Nieferxis Creative Works
5116 Bissonnet St. #459
Bellaire Tx 77401

ACKNOWLEDGMENTS

To my creators

Whose inspiration remains Timeless……

Thanks to my family and friends

For their feedback.

About The Author

With all of our new technology, where is the morality in making these decisions when/how to use it. ?

There is none--except $$$

RapperMD practices in Texas.
A nephrologist.
Kidney disease is growing fast nationwide.
The majority of the patients are from two major ethnic groups
   .... african americans
   .... mexican americans

¡ Therefore some of the information es en español !

The following is based on real accounts with patients over the past 10 years.

Time to enlighten, but for me
...time to cry

CATHARSIS

Acknowledgements.......4

About the Author.....5

I Rapper Who? 09

Rapper who..12; An overview of the kidney...12

II Process of Healing 21

Scars.....24; Compliance....28; HIV Nephropathy..30

III Minerals, Rocks 32

No difference...34; Calciphylaxis...36

IV Pobre Nutrición 39

Escúchame...41; Tex-Mex...44; My emotional pleas #4...46; To the children..49

Catharsis continues…..

V Control 51

Liars + hypocrites #1…54; Mento-nomic recession….59; Reuse….66

VI Who Are You? 69

Liars + hypocrites #2…..72; Makin' rounds…74; Pimps + ho's #1…78; Pimps + ho's #2…80; Memo..82

VII Emotional Pleas 84

Azúcar song…86; Para repasar…89; 'Watar-watar'..90; No áigre'…92

Poems Copyright 2007…95

Chapter I

Rapper Who?

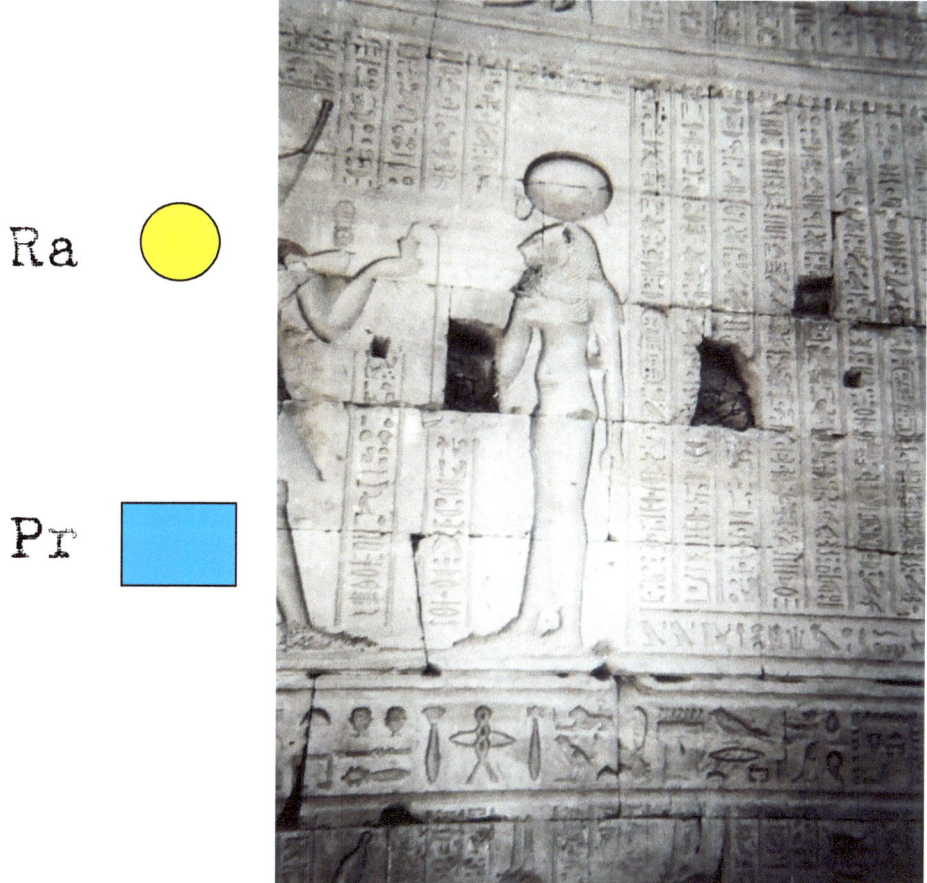

Ra 🟡

Pr 🟦

'House of Ra'

RAPPER WHO?

I'm a healthcare professional NOT knowing

what to do.

Frustrated by this healthcare system.

It's shit.

It affects me and you.

To pay such a high premium for us fortunate

to have a job

Just to see services DENIED, insurance rules dictated by

fat slobs.

This is MY OPINION, how I see things unfold.

Some say arrogant, some say angry......others

just say bold.

Capitalistic greed in a country that should

be great.

Lyin' that they care, lyin' cause they're fake.

rapper who....

None of this is new. You've heard
this before.
But what can be done? We remain spiritually,
physically and/or financially poor......

So I write, play music, practice
this medicine game.........
For what? To keep my soul n mind from
Goin' insane.

What a sad way to obtain wealth.
What a sad way to obtain fame.

That's my emotional plea.......
That's why I'm RAPPER MD.

An Overview of the Kidneys--

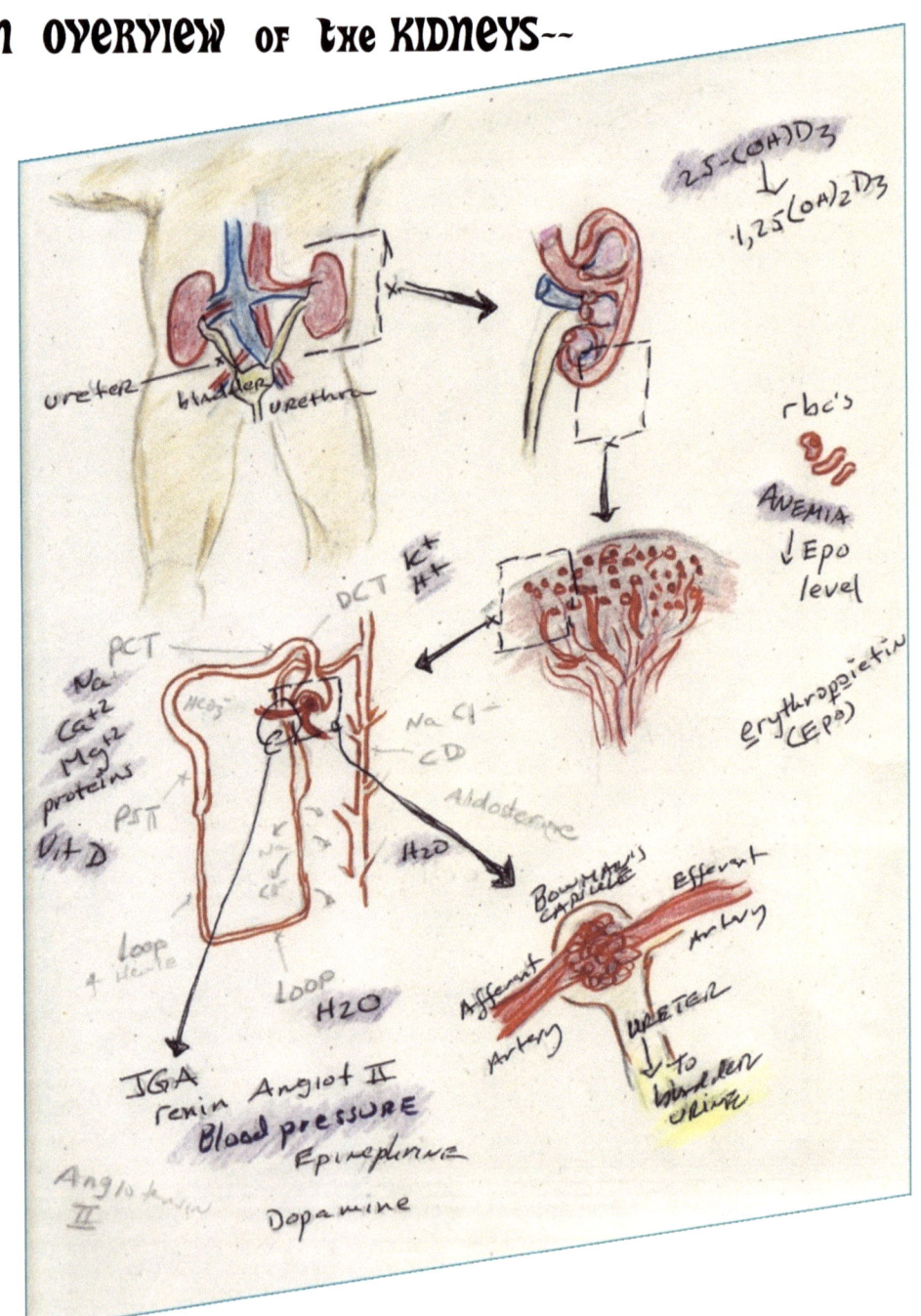

1—It makes water (H_2O) +

Regulates minerals like sodium (Na^+)

Magnesium (Mg^{+2})   Hydrogen (H^+)

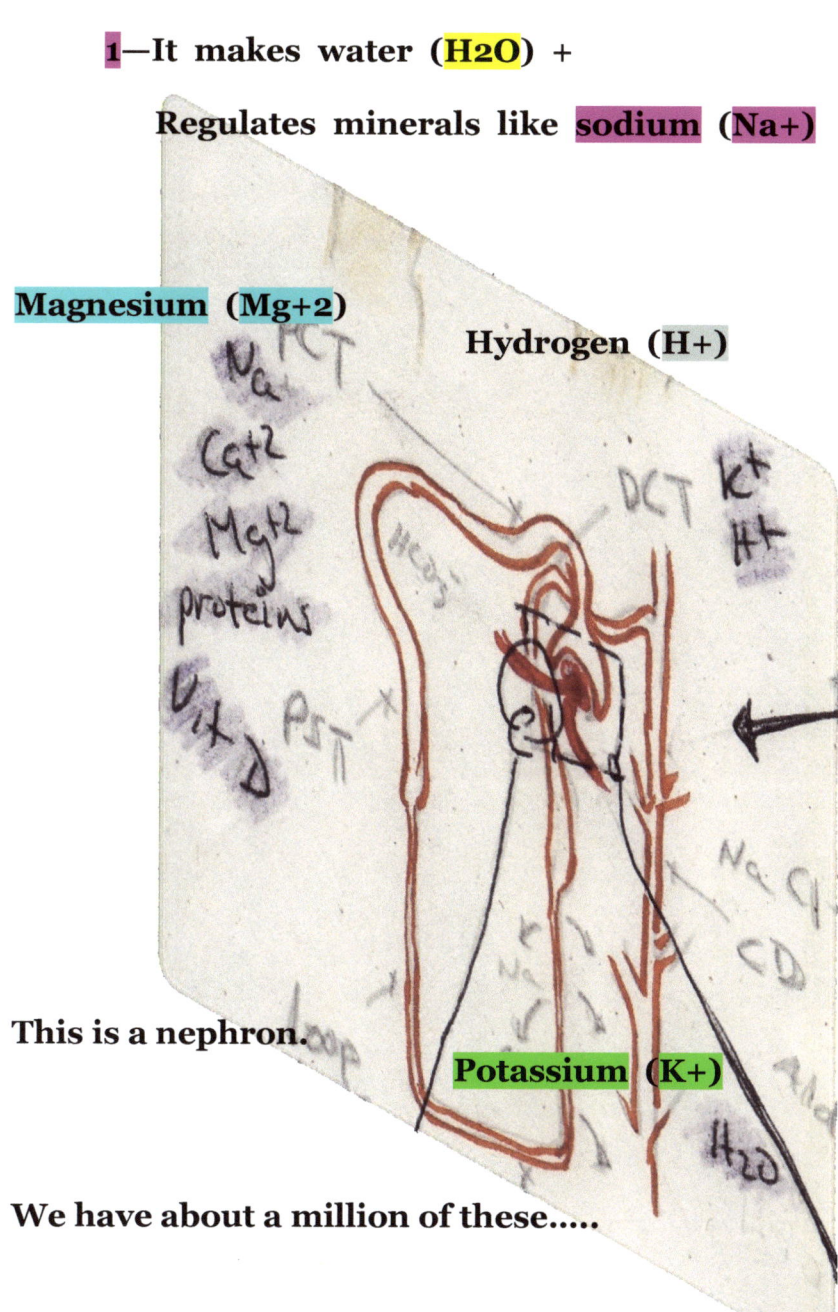

This is a nephron.

Potassium (K^+)

We have about a million of these.....

- Copyright © 2010 by RapperMD

2-Just like a filter, it cleans the blood and removes toxins

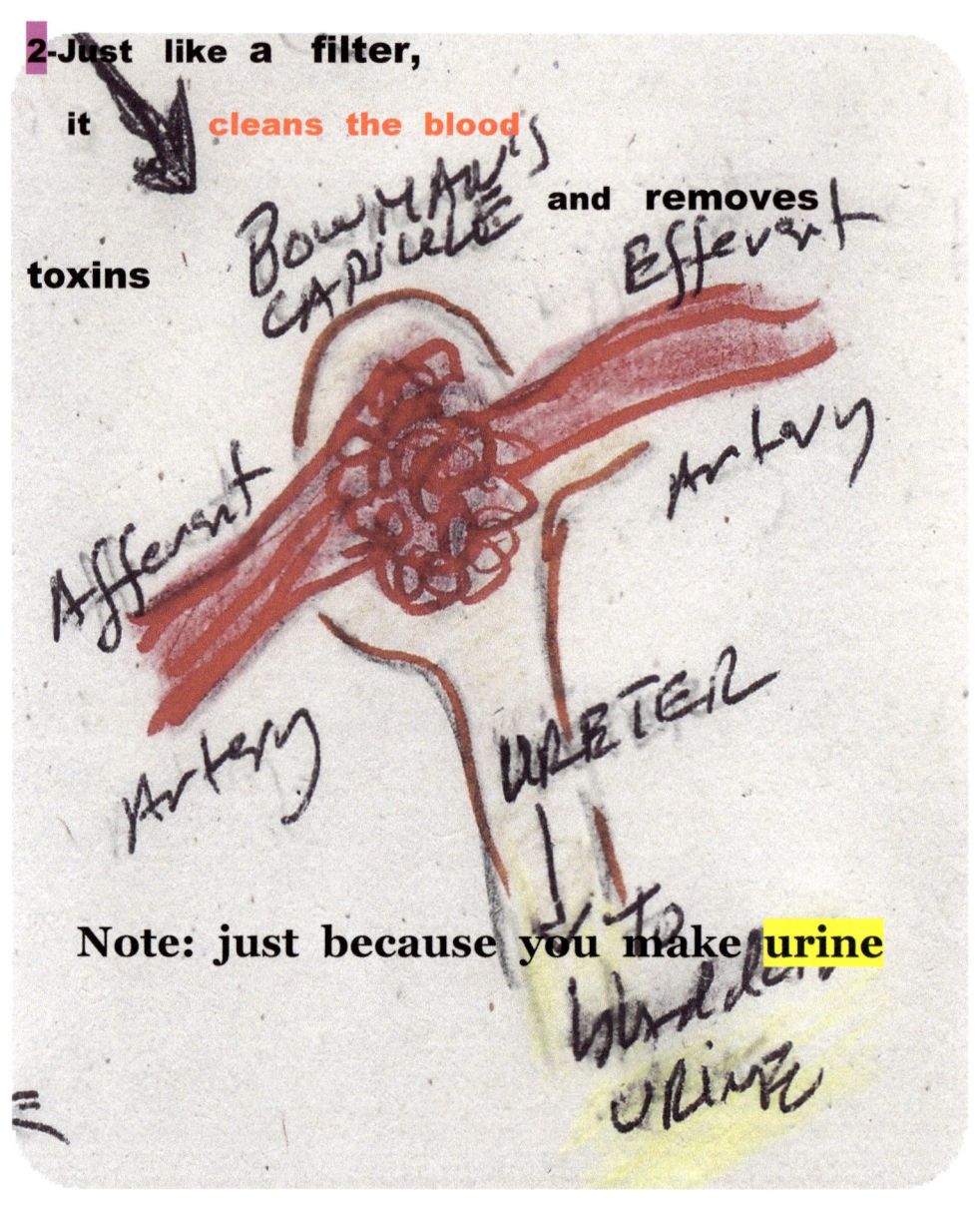

Note: just because you make urine

...doesn't mean your blood is clean!

....**3**..its makes Erythropoietin.

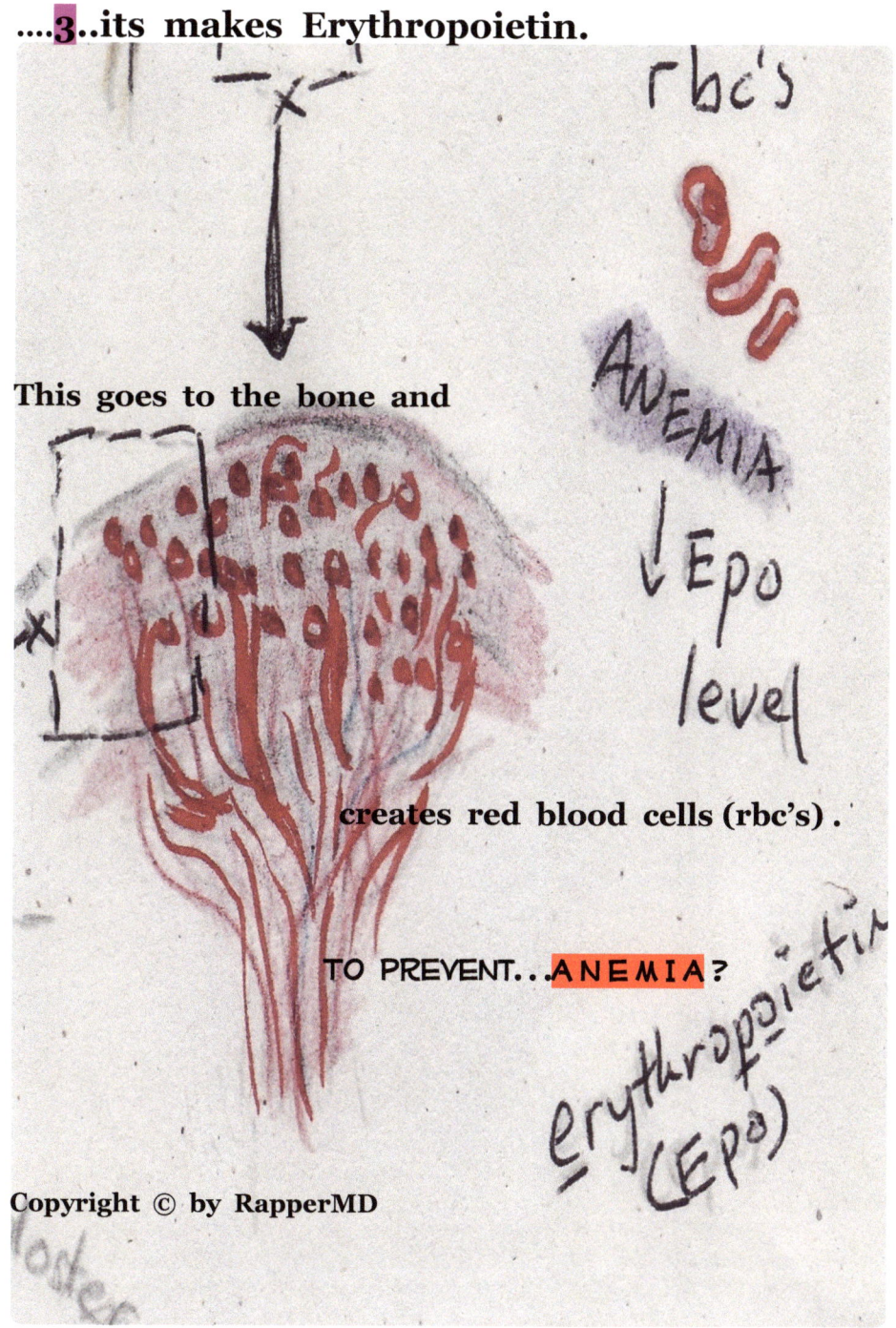

This goes to the bone and creates red blood cells (rbc's).

TO PREVENT...ANEMIA?

Copyright © by RapperMD

4....it activates vitamin D.

Remember your calcium (Ca+2)

and your phosphorus (PO4)

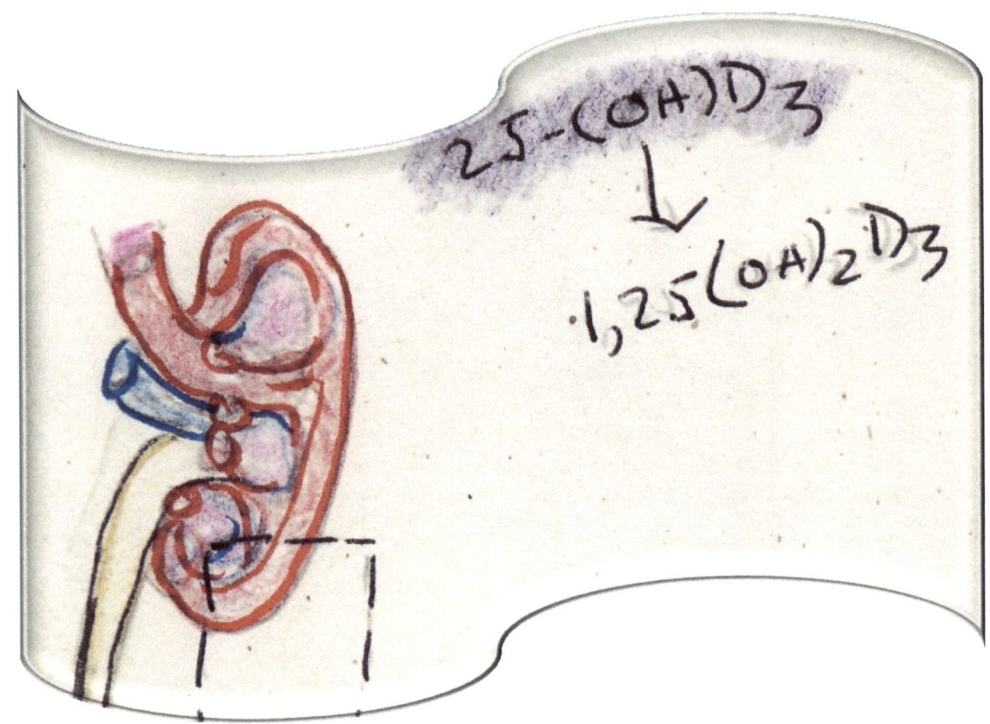

for those strong bones ?

copyright © by RapperMD

...5...it regulates your blood pressure!

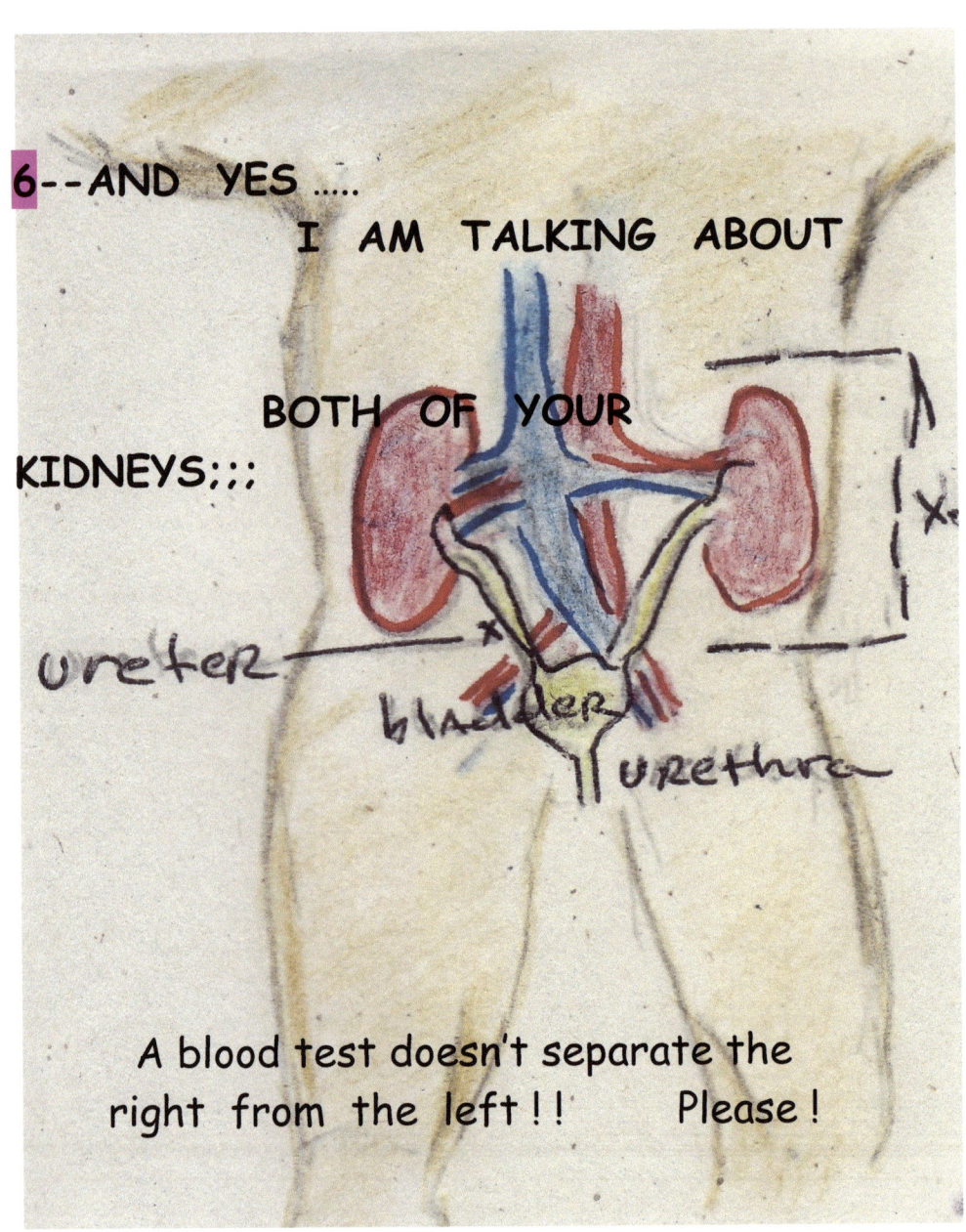

.....I HAVE BEGGED AND PLEADED...

ASK YOUR FAMILY TO COME AND SUPPORT YOU.

※

※

※

BUT HELL, THEY'RE JUST AS FATTT....

AND HAVE DIABETES TOO!.....

Chapter II

The Process of Healing

Scars...written 2007....pg24

Compliance..written 11-23-06.....pg26

HIV Nephropathy ..written 10-7-09.....
   to all the 'Aunt Evelyns'...pg30

We heard of the 'immune system'. It's the way our body prevents disease and heals itself.

By system, there are many avenues to accomplish this...

Cells from bone marrow

Cells from lymphatic glands

Cells from the wall lining our blood vessels...

Etc...

There are cells from blood vessel walls called fibroblasts.

This leads to scar tissue.

Scar tissue---- >no blood flow---- >DEATH to whichever/whatever structure(s) not receiving blood on the other end!

SCARS

We suffer from battle scars.

Mental scars

Vaginal and rectal scars....

Over active fibroblast cells...fibrosis tissues...

covering our many injuries

So much scar tissue that we can't even pee.

Scars that make us hard and ready to fight,

Scar up the renal arteries ....dialysis day n night.

Scar up our brains...our thoughts are now wack,

scars…..

Scar up our heart…arrthymias, heart attacks..

Scar up our skin…forming keloids lookin' like our African kinsmen

Scars from the beginning and scars to the end!

COMPLIANCE

Your arteries are like tubes or like pipes
They run to your kidneys
ALL DAY and ALL NIGHT.
Now you are hook up to an artificial one
And you want to cut your time down some?

You know you ate shit
Now you smell like shit
Waste products gives your skin itching fits!

You claim 'the doctors never explained it to me......
@ least not in the way you do.'
I say, 'no...you thought that it just wouldn't happen to you!

Clean up your act and do the right thang.
My words run true, so your heart does pain.

It's too late for you
but not for the little ones...
Show them by example and
not by your lying tongue!.......

...I am woman.

Created by thy lord god.

And you still don't know what to do with your

'Fishing rod '?

Lettin' your cowardness threaten my life.

Cuttin' to my soul like a knife....

When a person gets

HIV/AIDS from sexual contact. . . .

Other sexual transmitted diseases

GO ALONG FOR THE RIDE!!!

. . . . herpes

----> warts

. . . .hepatitis B,C---------- > leads to liver

---->cirrhosis/cancer.

HIV NEPHROLOGY

This is a real disease.

Gang raped in prison

while showering or trying to sleep.

Or your man lying to you 'bout where his thang

has been…

He had it in someone's BUTT!!

Now he wants you to 'scream his name!'

Baby baby, baby, why do I have hepatitis B?

My kidneys are fucked up,

I'm on a dialysis machine.

I smell like piss, my eyes are all yellow

My belly swollen, breath stanks,

liver cirrhosis……Hell---low!

You stick your dick in shit,

Then put it in me.

Now I have HIV Nephro-pathy!

You fucked up
bastard,
Our children hear
me crying.
You fucked up
bastard, I'm slowly
dying.•

Chapter III

Minerals, Rocks

NO DIFFERENCE...WRITTEN IN
1996__PG 34

CALCIPHYLAXIS...WRITTEN 2007
__...PG 36

NO DIFFERENCE

Crack cocaine? Powder or rocks?
The caffeine in your coffee,
Palpates that heart.
Candy, pies, cakes.....you eat these....
Yeah, you do!
Isn't granulated fine sugar.....white powder too?

It's all white powder,
All three are the same.
Processed/refine in chemistry labs
Is how they got there names!

Crack-----hardens the arteries,
Caffeine----elevates blood pressure,
Sugar so high.....we can't even measure!

They make you feel good
They make you feel high.
Hide if you want to
'cause blood test don't lie!

no difference.....

Old school, new school...
TRUE SCHOOL...yeah that's me ,
You'll be hook up to more
Than just a dialysis machine!!!!!

●

CALCIPHYLAXIS

Now you are on your death bed,

A penny for your thoughts of what's going through your head.

Family at your side, Doctors, med students at what USE to be feet

The docs explaining to them the importance of the food you choose to eat.

She shows them the stumps where they use to be hands,

She pulls back the sheets….you're no longer a man!

'Calciphylaxis' the med student answers.

Doc says 'correct'.

The lack of your binders you continue to neglect.

Yes phosphorus comes from your Coke, snacks and most food,

calciphlaxis......

But you kept eating whatever the hell you wanted to !
'Where are your phosphate binders? ' she'll ask on her rounds,
You look her in the eye....'mi truck'....with disgust and a frown.

Calciphylaxis, yes that's the term.
What's left of your body is barely enough food for worms.
Family members sobbing, they have tears in their eyes.
You think you are still living,
But to them you've already died.

So you close your eyes...this may be your last day,
One final glance, one final say....

calciphylaxis.....

..."So as I lay down my head to sleep, the doctors words I did not heed,
nor yours Lord did I keep.
Please let me come home.....if not for my soul's sake,
And let my death teach my family not to make the same mistakes!
Amen." ∎

Chapter IV

Pobre Nutrición

Escúchame escrito 12-02-06

Tex-Mex escrito 11-09-06

My Emotional Plea #4 2007

To The Children written 5-4-09

ESCÚCHAME

Mire se usted en un espejo.

Estás tan gordo, que té tengo miedo.

Camina como un elefante,

Con ropa no parece elegante.

Los jóvenes parecen lo mismo

Comiendo comida mala....con tú ejemplo.

Los niños no pueden correr, ni puedan respirar.

¡Qué lástima cuando jóvenes con la mala salud

....no pueden jugar!

Cuándo niños tienen senos y panzas

grandiosas....

¡Parecen como mujeres, parecen

embarazadas!

Yo sé que están comiendo papas fritas....

¡Pan dulces, huevos rancheros y empanadas!

escúchame....

Sí McDonald's es nuestro lugar,
Cuando estás en el hospital, ¿quién va
a pagar?
¿Pagar por tú insulina, agujas y syringes?
Para controlar tú azúcar......ya tiene diabetes.

¿Y porqué sigues comiendo cualquiera cosa?
Un ataque cerebral/ a el corazón... i tú
presión es alta.!
Te quejas de los problemas íntimos
pero tus riñones no elimina tóxicos.
Estos problemas- - - sexuales....
¡Ya necesitas diálisis!

Dejas el cuerpo sufrir con esta destrucción.
Por tú pobres escogidos; i es tú pobre
nutrición!

escúchame....

Muestra a tú familia hábitos nuevos
y buenos,
Estas enfermedades son secundo de la dieta.....poco genéticos.

Es importante de cambiar nuestra manera de vivir.
¡Escucha mi voz......no quieres morir! ∎

TEX-MEX

Catfish, shrimp, organs that contain shit!
And you want to know why you're not physically fit?

So a man thinketh, so is he,
So a women cooketh, she feeds the whole FAT family.

You weigh in @ 252,
Your creatinine is 2.2.
172 is your sugar. And you 'Wobble', not walk.....
You big fat *^@#/*+!

You disrespect me in the office,
Have resentment in your eyes....
You turn your head and look away from me
And mumble 'we all goin' die'!

Well kill yourself you fool, I'll make money off of you.
And when your ass is in the hospital....
The other doctors will too!

45   tex-mex ....

Oh let's not forget our menudo eatin' cuzins',
They come to dialysis by the dozens!

Estamos lo mismo, tú español......mi inglés.
Se cambia, se maltrata a través de 'CONQUEST'.

Se cambia nos religión, nos idioma, nos comida.....
Tanta grase, cosas fritas, no es tan buena.

Tapa las arterias, no puede pensar,
Tapa el pene........no trabajar.
Sí lo usa en un modo tan cariñoso,
Probable la señora cocina cosas mas bueno!

Tenemos cambia nos manera de vida.
¡Escucha me voz....escucha me grita! ▪

MY EMOTIONAL PLEA #4

Hay un problema...
Con los mercados, los restaurantes y las tiendas
Cuando se venden cosas que no son buenas.

No es bueno para la salud.
No es bueno para el espíritu.
Se causa destrucción, muerte y solitud.

Se venden frutas tan temprano para comer.
Se inyectan químicos en los animales para crecer.
Crecen rápido, muy rápido y los inmovilizan.. ..
En una manera ruda, se los matan.

En un modo tan horrible,
Se cambia la genética de las frutas y vegetables.
Eso no es suficiente....
Tenemos que comprar ¡vitaminas o suplementes.!

my emotional plea....

No es bueno para la salud.
No es bueno para el espíritu.
Se causa destrucción, muerte y solitud.

El viento, la tierra, incluyendo el agua,
Con respecto y honor…... mi gente les adora.
Pero ustedes manchan y siguen riendo…..
Necesitamos estas cosas para vivir. ... ¡Por dinero , que tonto .!

No tiene interés en las consecuencias de
su acción...
Sigue con los venenos en su destrucción.

Algunos de estos productos producen.....'drogadición '.
Entonces..SE PONE MAS en los productos.. ...
Usted es la culpa de nuestra desmoralización.

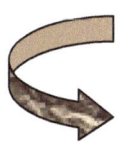

my emotional plea …..

No le damos información…..
Hasta que hay muertes……..las leyes esfuerzan una investigación.
Con sus tóxicos crean nuevas enfermedades….
Obesidad, sida….con mentiras se dice…
… . .. ¿ Pero no sabe ?

Hay niños con senos, niñas con bebes
Enfermedades de los riñones, del corazón
y diabetes.

No es bueno para la salud.
No es bueno para el espíritu.
Se causa destrucción, muerte y solitud. ∎

TO THE CHILDREN

Parental supervision is recommended
Cause what you
'bout to hear
they will be offended.

By their actions they're teaching you
How to be a fat slob too.
(uh-uh........)

Flip the script, crack the genetic string
Be pickin' what u put n your mouth
Quality things.
Family will like what they see
And maybe follow you.
Normal cholesterol no diabetes

A healthier sexy you! ■

...Your poor diet choices is why you sit in this chair....

You still don't listen to me, you look away and stare....

Are you staring towards heaven? 'cause that's where you'll soon be. Leaving behind another empty seat.

It will be filled by another!

Very quickly!....

Chapter V   *Control*

Liars + Hypocrites #1, written 5-28-07…. Pg 54

Mento-nomic Recession, written 3-15-09 pg 59

Reuse. .written 6-6-09..pg 66

THE VERY SOURCE OF OUR LIFE

CONTROL BY INDIVIDUALS WHO ONLY WANT

TO MAKE A FAST BUCK!

Liars and Hypocrites #1

Organize the masses,
Education for all classes.

I think this is cultural design
The poorest (now middle class people) will have to decline….
The healthier, natural foods…not present in their hoods.
It's fast fried burgers, pizzas, high salt and sugar- laden foods.

Is this a form of gradual extinction?
Clearly death is link with health is linked with nutrition.

Soldiers checking e-mails , children with cell phones.
Engineering plant cells with animal cells, do you
hear mother nature's groans?
Prisoners with internet access, hi- definition-TV.
Explain to me how malnutrition can equate with obesity?

Where mental and physical growth retard while in the
 wombs of our mothers.
There still exist malnutrition, vitamin deficiency…
death in high numbers!!
Beriberi, scurvy, kwashiorkor, leprosy.
Pellagra, malarial waters, high infant mortalities!

liars and hypocrites #1…..

Genetic inferiority? Gradual extinction:
Clearly death is link with health is linked to our nutrition.

There is no morality with all this new technology.
The developments are done fast, get the people hooked…
to make quick money.
No consequences of actions does one consider.
Toxic garbage shot up into space or placed in hoods/countries
populated by x+!:>>??

Medical conferences ask..why kidney disease in blacks is so high?
Restricted income , bias education, fucked up water..food supply!
So when we are born, we're already behind?
Less cells in our organs? Ineffective immune system?
We drop like flies…we die!

REMIX:
We quickly form scar tissue. Making ourselves hard n' tough.
That's how we fight.
But when there's scar tissue in our kidneys, what's offer is
dialysis day or all night!   ~~~▶

liars and hypocrits #1 …

Scar tissue in our brains..makes our thoughts wack.
Scar tissue in the heart…means big fat heart attack.

Is this a genetic design? Fuckin' with our minds?
Fuckin ' with our existence? Clearly death is link with health.
Nutrition is where we need medical assistance!

How do we change the conditions for ALL of our advancement?
How do we change our way of thinking? For our survival?
...for our planet? ●

Mento-nomic Recession

In this time of yet another 'economic' recession, with info technology that affords the exposure of LIARS to millions of people……..
    it's not just the lies of material wealth,
    but the lies of our food,
    water….life itself…………

Now that I'm an adult, dependent on liars for my FOOD.
Grocery stores restaurants, non-domestic farmers…….what a FOOL!

Even I'm guilty of not learning this SKILL, tilling the soil, planting seeds in the FIELDS.

mento-nomic recession.....

FOR MY OWN HEALTH, LIFE CAN BE CRUEL. BUT A GOOD LIFE IS WEALTH....WHAT A FOOL!

Not knowing what's injected in the food I BUY!
 Not knowing what was sprayed on it...
STUPID ME I CRY!
 Disodium inosinate, caramel color, reading labels, packages and THANGS.....

FOR MY OWN HEALTH LIFE CAN BE CRUEL. BUT A GOOD LIFE IS WEALTH I SANG!

'Not tested in animals' is to make me feel GOOD? Or labeled 'natural' or 'organic' means the food is COOL?

mento-nomic recession....

Organic means carbon-based, the building block of our LIVES.
 But industry's greed is destroying us, so I guess we deserve to DIE?

Now you are exposed LIARS! We want to grow our own FOOD. But if you're program for something else......you don't know how TO.

FOR MY OWN HEALTH, LIFE CAN BE CRUEL. BUT GOOD FOOD IS WEALTH. YOU DON'T LEARN THIS IN SCHOOL.

Genetically alter seeds to plant in non-fertile GROUNDS! Growin' n garden engineerin' soil, hangin' n the air, ➡

mento-nomic recession...

...tomato vines grown upside DOWN!
Or vegetables grown from a bowl, that doesn't even need SUN!
 Your gut says 'that's weird' as children we played outdoors....sometimes in mud....that
 was FUN!

Instinct, curiosity, as children we played
in that DIRT.
Dug up earthworms, caterpillars, bugs...
...LIFE.....MOTHER EARTH.

But I didn't want to grow up messin' around n the ground.

mento-nomic recession.....

A new lesson:

    what u don't know will HURT.

    I should of mastered the 'art of soil'....

    what one can do with DIRT.

For knowledge like seeds I did not SOW.

My own food, water, to liars I OWE.

My energy, my very life....as a commodity.

Bought and sold.......

FOR MY OWN HEALTH LIFE CAN BE CRUEL,

BUT A GOOD LIFE IS WEALTH.

WHAT A FOOL. ♦

.....and when I come to you

with facts.. straight.....

You grab a lawyer

and direct at me hate.....

A common practice is

to reuse the artificial kidney(filter)

when giving patients their dialysis treatments.

Patients are scared when they begin their treatments.

They rely on their doctors to make the best decision for them.

To use a new filter OR a used one.

They are given . . . .

informed consent?

@ the time of this publication....some dialysis clinics are doing away with this. They are using a new/ sometimes called 'dry pack'. After 10+ years of REUSE!

Is this because of patients safety?

Or $$??$$??......

REUSE

Do you reuse needles or re-chew old gum?
Do you rinse and cleanse, then reuse your tampon?

We question why patients have
low kt over V's.
So what we do.... increase the QB.
Now let's increase sitting time.
Is all this necessary to save a dime?

Yes it's expensive to care for
the sick and poor.
What % is that of the Medicare budget?
I can't take these lies no more.

Like a Ponzi scheme there is no new
wealth to pay.
Scheming in board rooms, lie and say....
"We need a plan for this, a committee for
that...,
It cost this amount".. as we add to
our debt! -- --▶▶

I DON'T KNOW WHAT IS THE RIGHT ANSWER.
SELFISHNESS AND GREED IS GROWING LIKE A CANCER.

WHAT GOES AROUND COMES AROUND YES IS AN OLD CLICHÉ.
WHO'S GOING TO STAND BY ME, TO HELP IN MY LAST DAYS?

SO I ASK..DO WE REUSE NEEDLES? WE REUSE HOSPITAL GOWNS.
REUSE DIALYZE FILTERS? THEY LOOK LIKE REUSED GIANT TAMPONS!
REUSE BANDAGES? WE REUSE HOSPITAL SHEETS.
ALL TO SAVE LIVES OR MONEY? SINCE HEALTH CARE IS NOT CHEAP! ■ ■

Chapter VI

WHO

are

  **YOU?**

Liars + Hypocrites #2, written 5-28-07…pg72

Makin' Rounds, written 2008 ….pg 74

Pimps + Ho's #1, written 10-09 …..pg 78

Pimps + Ho's #2….pg80

Memo, written 1-08…pg82

.....Hum-mm-m –' business of health..',

I'm going' to choke!

Why do so many health care professionals

smell like

cigarette smoke ????...

....excerpt my emotional plea #3A

Liars + Hypocrites #2

Would you take your ride to a mechanic whose car never runs?
Go to a beautician whose hair is always undone?
So why see a doctor whose body ain't tight?
Snackin' on the run, so their breathe ain't right?

Looking sloppy + fat, laughing with coffee-stain teeth.
Breast stick out so much, they can't see their own 2 feet.
 OR
Belly stick out so much, they piss all over the toilet seat.

Do you really think they are goin' to cure you?
Why? Because they take medications too?

Hangin' out in the doctors lounge, complaining that the food is too bland!
Grabbing that salt shaker……shake, shake, shake,
You're a cardiologist man?

Some of you are gynecologist, nephrologist, various specialties.
Double chin, bustin' thru your lab coat..
You're treating people……people who can't pee?

"We're trying to get small ……just like you…."
Well first you can start off by washing your damn hands…yeah over there . . . . .there's the bathroom!

Hospital events, many gifts, eatin' all that free food…
The more people we put in this place, that's more money for me, the hospital. . . . .
yeah that's real good!!··

MAKIN' ROUNDS

Dietician:

When that fat dietician wobbles over towards your machine
Telling you your calcium is high from
milk or ice cream.

I can see it in your eyes....see it in
your face,
You know that fat fool is out of place......

The hypocrisy to preach to you
About healthy living.
Who in the hell do you think she/he is kiddin'.

MD:

Here you come stumping towards me
you fat pig.

makin' rounds . . . .

Can't even button your lab coat.
Your gut is too big.

Claiming to be a doctor. You don't
Follow your own advice . . . .
Your recommendations are questionable.
I'm callin' Miami Vice!

'Arrest this person for identity theft.'
Impersonating a healthcare professional,
Being fat yourself . . . . . . ••...

{police sirens}

What's my desire.

No longer for hire.

I'm heading for the door

I mean it...I'm leavin—leavin—

Leaving…………. . .

PIMPS + Hos #1

We went into medicine hoping to cure the world.....
Demand for us to respond to your emergency
Last to be paid 'cause it's NOT YOUR URGENCY'

Rules and regulations made by MD's ('He retired when?').
The hours demand by us you think we were machines.

It took years of study to master our trade
Workin' many long hours, everyone else gets paid!

All those years to become a **MEDICARE HO!**
Pimp by drug companies, insurances rules, PP and HMO's...

You pimp tellin me how to conduct my practice,
what words to use,
Where the hell I can go.

pimps + ho's #1....

Pushing your chemicals, reimbursement for cheap tests,
It is still about control-----

Like organize drug lords, gang bangers, you talk about
 territory and money.....
"I'm sorry it's only business", paid by whom?....
this ain't funny!!!!!. ▪ ▪

{shoutin n background...'get back to work b*^#@!!!}

PIMPS + Hos #2

PIMP:

We cover ALL the hospitals in the city,

Yes including those long term facilities.

OFFICE-Double + triple book patients so that waiting room is pack. Check x-rays, check labs...

Yes patients want you to call them back.

Don't be late

Don't be wrong

Don't keep the patient waiting too long.....

HO:

Work work work

No sleep

No life

pimps + ho's #2.......

No   family

No fun

Work work work

From night 'til dawn.●●

Memo

Elections are soon, so you are a politician again.
Lying, promising, saying whatever to get in.....
Pretending to care about people's health!
Our tax dollars gone/goin' to war.....
which is death!

Elections are near, so you're playing a politician?
Claiming to care about health,
global warming, college tuition?

What about nutrition. Is this an issue with you?
Why allow industries to place so much sugar
in teas, cereal, so called 'healthy foods'?

Saving the planet to you is a joke.....
You still don't know what water is.
Selling a 'flavored' now - color – citric- acid –
version of coke!

memo . . .

There exist internet with global information documentaries confirming these points about health, events leading to 9-11, capitalism.......

I think the problem is the privilege few.
The rich/greedy ones, who control our countries, building weapons of mass destruction? . . . . .
Telling governments what to do!

Some claim that they are the 1 %, or others call them the Talented - Few.
From all walks of life they are.....
rich.....or....asians.....brown....white.....atheists
...or.. ...jews!!!

Like 'animal planet' it's survival of the fittest.

WE ARE NOT CIVILIZED AT ALL............Ω

Chapter VII

VII   My Emotional Pleas

VII My Emotional Pleas

Azúcar, Azúcar written 12-27-09

Water, Water written 12-29-09

No aire written 12-28-09

AZÚCAR SONG 12-27-09

Estoy pensando en ustedes.

Pero mi mensaje no tiene interés.

Trato de presentar lo diferente

No lo aguanto, no quiere.

♪♪   ♪♪   ♪♪

Ideas de cocinar, ideas de jugar.

Cuando faltan sus riñones,

No tiene relaciones. Su cosa no trabaja.

Y necesita viagra. Eso no es suficiente

¡Ya tiene diabetes!

Estoy pensando en ustedes. Mi mensaje no oyen.

Estos secretos dolorosos, tratan de esconder.

Este estilo de vida ; ¡es la manera de morir.!

Ideas de cocinar, ideas de jugar.

No tiene vergüenza en las consecuencias.

azúcar, azúcar......

Cuándo falta su riñón, se queja de comezón.
A mí no me creas. ¡Ya tiene diabetes!
♪♪
Azúcar, azúcar ....¿ porqué me luchan ?
Azúcar, azúcar......¿ porqué me gritan ?
Azúcar , azúcar... . ¿ de quién es la culpa .?
A mí no me escuchan.... azúcar.
Sus medicinas ¿ dónde están ? ..azúcar.
Su presión es alta.....azúcar.
¡Y colesterol es alto!

Con esta enfermedad.......
...pierde sus ojos....... ¡NO VISTA!
Pierde sus dedos..... ¡NO MANEJA!
Pierde sus piernas...... ¡NO CAMINA!
Y arteria cerebrales..... ¡NO HABLA!
Se come cosas con grasa.........¡Gorditas!
Se come cosas fritas.........¡camarones!

azúcar, azúcar....

Come cosas de piel........¡chicharrones!
Cosas con miel............¡y pan dulce!
Se come cosas malas.......
¡No Es Mí Culpa!

Azúcar, azúcar .... ¿porqué me luchan?
Azúcar, azúcar.......a mí no me escuchan.
Azúcar, azúcar.......su peso sube...
Azúcar, azúcar...... ¡tiene diabetes!

Azúcar......sus medicinas faltan..... .azúcar
Su colesterol es alto.... . ..azúcar
Su presión es alta..... ...azúcar
¿Porqué me luchan?..... .azúcar.
A mí no me escuchan. .... azúcar, azúcar♪

Um-mmmmm....¡ES MI LUCHA.!

-----Los riñones...

1-- producen agua y regular minerales como sodio, fosforo, potasio, ...

2— eliminar tóxicos pues limpia el sangre....

Nota: aunque puede orinar, no es igual que la sangre esta limpia...

3— participar en la formación de vitamina D. Este ayuda en la dura de los huesos.

4— se producen erythropoietin. Un químico que asiste en la formación de los glóbulos rojos.

5— controlar la presión arterial....

6—y estoy hablando de ambos riñones......

Copyright © by RapperMD

'WATAR WATAR'

WHY YOU KEEP DRINKING ALL THIS WATER
(YOU CAN NOT PEE)
YOU KNOW YOU JUST GOING TO DROWN.
(YOU CAN NOT PEE)
WHY YOU KEEP DRINKING ALL THIS WATER
(YOU CAN NOT PEE)
YOU KNOW YOU JUST GOING TO DROWN, DROWN

YOUR KIDNEYS DO NOT WORK
(WHERE IS IT GOING TO GO)
A LITTLE MORE YOU SAY WON'T HURT
(WHERE IS IT GOING TO GO)
FOOD AND WATER KEEPS POURING DOWN
(WHERE IS IT GOING TO GO)
BURY YOURSELF RIGHT IN THAT GROUND

MORE WATER , MORE WATAR, MORE WATER,......

YOU WONDER WHY
(YOU KEEP ON FEELING SICK)
YOU EATING ANIMALS

(ANIMALS THAT EAT SHIT)
AND ADD MORE TABLE SALT
(THAT'S WHY YOU'RE THOWING UP)

♪   ♪ ♪ ♪   ♪

YOUR CHEST IS TIGHT, CAN'T TAKE NO MORE
YOU CAN NOT BREATHE, YOU FALL AND HIT THE FLOOR
KEEP WONDERING WHY YOU FEELING SICK
KEEP ON DRINKING WATER, AND NEVER QUIT.

MORE WATER , MORE WATAR, MORE WATER. . .

♪   ♪ ♪ ♪   ♪

ALL THAT FOOD YOU PILLING HIGH
(PILLING HIGH UP ON YOUR PLATE)
A TRIPLE BYPASS WILL SOON
(WILL SOON BE YOUR FATE)
AND PRETTY SOON YOU CAN NOT PEE
(SO YOU SPEND ALL YOUR TIME)
HOOKED UP TO A MACHINE

MORE WATER (WA-TAR). MORE WATER, MORE WATAR. . . ..

NO AIRE   (TEX-MEX DICE 'NO AIGRE')

COMIDA CON TANTA SAL
¿NO SABES PORQUÉ TE SIENTES MAL?
CUÁNDO SE CONECTAS A LA MÁQUINA
TANTOS CALAMBRES ¡QUÉ LÁSTIMA!

DEMASIADO AGUA
EL RESPIRO TE FALTA.

NO AIRE (AIGRE), NO AIRE (AIGRE)....."ESTÓY
AHOGANDO".
NO AIRE (AIGRE) NO AIRE (AIGRE),......" RESPIRE
PROFUNDO".

¿TIENES SED? SANDÍA, MANGO Y JUGO TROPICALES,
TANTO QUÉ BEBER.
LA CANTIDAD QUÉ IGNORAS, AFECTA COMO VIVIR.
NO LIMITAS TUS LÍQUIDOS
NO PUEDES ORINAR. ¡QUÉ ESTUPIDO!
¿ADÓNDE VA TODA ÉSTE AGUA?
EL AIRE TE FALTA.

¿QUIERES ESTAR SANO?
¡CÚIDADO CON TÚ MANO!

NO AIRE (AIGRE), NO AIRE (AIGRE)......
' ESTOY AHOGANDO.'
NO AIRE (AIGRE), NO AIRE (AIGRE)....... ¡RESPIRE PROFUNDO!

EN DIÁLISIS MIDE TÚ PESO.
DOS PUNTO DOS ES UN KILO.
TRAES MAS DE OCHO LIBRAS. RÁPIDO RÁPIDO EL CORAZÓN BOMBEA.
Y CUANDO TÚ PRESIÓN ARTERIA SE BAJA.
'ME SIENTO PESADO'........PÁLPITA, PÁLPITA.

¿Y NO SABES PORQUÉ TE SIENTES MAL?
TANTAS COMIDA FRITA, LÍQUIDO Y SAL..

NO AIRE (AIGRE), NO AIRE (AIGRE),.....
" ESTÓY AHOGANDO ".
NO AIRE (AIGRE), NO AIRE (AIGRE), ... 'RESPIRE PROFUNDO!'

♪ ♪   ♪ ♪

SODIO, FOSFORO, MELÓN DE AGUA.
PIERNAS HINCHADAS, ¿SON PIES? O ¿SON PATAS?

TANTO POTASIO...¡AGUACATE!
COCINAS CON MANTECA.........¡TUS TAMALES!
¿QUIERES ALGO DULCE?.....¡CHAMPURRADO!
TIRAS EN LA BASURA......¡TÚ GUÍA DE ALIMENTOS!

HAY MUCHO GRASA....¡EN MENUDO!
Y FRITA TUS TORTILLAS.....¡UMMMM BUÑUELO!
A MI NO ME PONES ATENCIÓN
COMES MAS DE UN........¡CHICHARRÓN!

TORTILLAS DE HARINA.....¡CON POZOLE!
CABEZA, CARNE DE CERDO......¡QUIERO MOLE!
CALDO, SODAS OSCURAS, CAFÉ Y TÉ
HARTO CON TÚ COMIDA
HARTO......YO SÉ......

NO AIRE (AIGRE), NO AIRE (AIGRE), TE ESTÁS AHOGANDO.
NO AIRE (AIGRE), NO AIRE (AIGRE), ¡OXÍGENO ESTÁS BUSCANDO!

CONTROLA LO QUÉ PONES EN TÚ BOCA.
¡CONTROLA CON ESTE RÍTMO DE SOCCA! ♪♪

Poems Copyright © 2007 by RapperMD

COMPLIANCE......26

NO DIFFERENCE.......34

CALCIPHYLAXIS.......36

ESCÚCHAME.........41

MY EMOTIONAL PLEA #4.........46

TEX-MEX...........44

Illustrations and excerpts by RapperMD

Photographs by rcprmd

…..But I must respect my **elders**,

So I've explained the nice way….

You just look at me and laugh…

"Baby…we're all goin' die one day" !

Well life is a choice and yes we all will die.

But isn't the quality of how you're living

A reflection of YOU or a LIE!……

RapperMD ∞